GROWTH

Growth

Poems
by
PETER FREEMAN

Adelaide Books
New York / Lisbon
2019

GROWTH
Poems
By Peter Freeman

Copyright © by Peter Freeman
Cover image by Mary Freeman

Cover design © 2019 Adelaide Books

Published by Adelaide Books, New York / Lisbon
adelaidebooks.org

Editor-in-Chief
Stevan V. Nikolic

All rights reserved. No part of this book may be reproduced in any manner whatsoever without written permission from the author except in the case of brief quotations embodied in critical articles and reviews.

For any information, please address Adelaide Books
at info@adelaidebooks.org
or write to:
Adelaide Books
244 Fifth Ave. Suite D27
New York, NY, 10001

ISBN-10: 1-950437-41-8
ISBN-13: 978-1-950437-41-2

Printed in the United States of America

Contents

Contents v
Acknowledgments vii
Foreword ix
Childhood 1
   First Memories 1
   Flower, Belt, and Birthmark 3
   The Dunny Can Man 5
   The Fight 7
   Bullies Vanquished 10
   The Pedal Car 11
   Confession 14
   The Kittens 16
   The Tree House 20
   Old Men in the Shadows 23
Puberty 27
   First Kiss 27
   Last Beating 29
   I Walk the Line 33
   Riding My Tanka Bike 37
Adolescence 39
   Home for Men 39
   Desolation 43
   Aftermath 45
   Funnel 47
   Beach of Belonging 48
   Island of Sand 50
Adulthood 53
   Conscription 53
   Jungle of Thoughts 55
   Night in Life 56
   The Charge 58
   Night with the Gypsies 60

Contents

    Last Rites 63
    White Witch Virginia 64
    River Bank 66
    Black Night 67
    Night on the Beach 68
    Life 69
    A Day in Spain 70

Maturity **73**
    The Race 73
    Southern Ocean 78
    Passage 82
    Expression 83
    Lover's Call 85
    Touch 87
    Relation of Being 89

Wisdom **91**
    A Gathering of Vanished Days 91
    Growth 93
    A Heart of Changes 94
    Boys Will Be Boys 96
    Unfulfilled 99
    Melancholy 101
    Four Horsemen 103
    Apocalypse 105
    Future Shock 107
    Friend 109
Images 111
About the Author 113

Acknowledgments

To my Grade eleven English teacher, Mr. Barry Brown, whose exciting and encouraging words, written in red ink at the bottom of my first fictional short story, gave me the confidence and courage to share a deeper meaning of our human experiences.

To the many others whose paths I crossed in my meandering quest to understand this beautiful and precious world, and who did not see a lump of coal, but a diamond in the rough: thank you for polishing off my edges and allowing me to reflect your beauty, refract your truth, and condense your passion into a lighthouse beam to guide others across these stormy times.

Foreword

We come into this world, complex yet unformed. As we experience life through the years, it shapes us and changes us. Throughout this process, there is a desire to control how we are affected by life's forces. We are all engaged in the same process of trying to make sense of our existence and our surrounding environment. Our biological, emotional, and intellectual needs drive us into the company of others, where we share our experiences, insights, wonderment, and the bewilderment of our lives.

We are story tellers.

We share our stories in so many ways: through art, songs, poems, prose, stories, and speeches. We strive to condense powerful emotional experiences into a kernel of beauty and intensity that we hope will act as a catalyst to change people close to us, and then ripple outwards into our communities, and ultimately the world.

We should tell our stories…we must tell our stories.

Our fragile world depends on us to protect it from the ravages of damaged beings that have acquired sufficient power to threaten our very existence, and unknowingly, theirs as well. We must create and build our culture from ourselves, moulding it through music, sculpture, paintings, poetry, novels, and video lest we succumb to the dominant consumptive culture imposed from above.

We must create.

Creative work does not burst forth fully formed but, like ourselves, starts newborn and develops slowly, gaining power and influence until it can speak to the powerful, the corrupt, the angry, and the hurt. Creations can speak loudly and softly. They can sooth a troubled elder and delight a wide eyed child. If we are not creative beings, who are we?

We are nothing without creativity.

The more we leave our core humanity and extend ourselves into a world of rich creation, the more we separate from those who are also extending themselves from the same human beginnings to follow their creative needs. In an expanding universe, galaxies of creative endeavour are moving further and further apart.

We must connect.

We need a unified field of ideas and expression to reconnect us in some other dimension. We need to be in our own space and in the space of other's as well. We need a quantum connection with each other.

This is a collection of poems arranged in approximate chronological order to illustrate the moulding of one's personality, attitudes and motivations from internal and external events, as one grows through the various phases of life.

Childhood

First Memories

An encounter with a prince

My first years of life were spent in a small fishing village on the southeastern coast of Queensland in Australia. My father owned the Laguna II, a motor vessel on which he had made a living transporting tourists up the Noosa River to Lake Cootharaba and the Coloured Sands, 200 metre high multi-coloured sand dunes dyed from iron oxides and other compounds.

He sold his motor vessel and built his first small home, high atop a hill that over looked the small but growing village of Noosa Heads. The house stood on stilts, typical of the "Queenslander" design of the era, and it had been named Pinevale. It was a design that helped keep the house cool during the hot tropical summers by allowing air to flow under the house, slowed by the vertical slatted boards around the perimeter of the stilt-like piles. Large downspouts directed the heavy monsoonal rainfall down from the roof and horizontally away from the house.

Iridescent green tree frogs with their sticky suction cap-like fingers would live in the horizontal sections of drainpipe where the residue of water from the last downpour would sustain them. I was three years old when I managed to reach in with my narrow arm and pluck one of the frogs out of the drain pipe. It was my first memory of the world, another person's reaction to my actions, and my subsequent ill understood feelings.

> I took froggie out of drainpipe,
> as green as green could be
> It squirmed and slithered all around
> and tried to climb up on me.

Childhood

Into my barrow I placed him quiet,
wheeled him 'round and 'round
Till mommy told me "Stop it!
Put him back where he'd been found."

I grabbed him firmly round the neck
and shoved him up the pipe.
He made a croak, his legs they jumped,
and my hand I gave a wipe.

I was sad, I'd lost a friend,
I did not understand.
Alone again, I roamed about
to marvel at this land.

Flower, Belt, and Birthmark

A five-year-old boy's experience with a priest

Many times during the first half-dozen years of my life, I was left in the care of people, some even strangers to my parents, as they went off to find work. For a couple of weeks during one summer, I was left in the care of the Catholic Brothers at St. Patrick's church in Gympie. While I was at St Patrick's, another boy my age taught me to tie my shoelaces as I had lived my life up to that point without wearing shoes, except while attending church, when my mother did it for me.

We were housed in a large dormitory and, at lights-out, the brothers would sit upon our cots to pray. One man took advantage of the opportunity it presented and took me to a separate room. The memories from that night were repressed for over thirty years until unearthed by a yellow light in a darkened room, similar to the scene I had witnessed as a boy. The identical matching of what I saw as a thirty-eight year old man with what I had seen as a five-year-old boy, triggered the connection and ripped that memory out of the depths of my brain. An anguished howl burst from me as all the buried experiences came pouring out.

What man of monstrous design
imposed on you a will so taken
with corruption and faithless guile
that took your newness fresh.

When his intent, unknown to you,
slid soundlessly into yellow room
weakly lit from a hangman's cord
and cap of purity above a baleful glare.

With nascent fear, you watched
his dark set shape beyond your feet.
Your legs, so bare atop the cloying sheet,
shrinking pillow into dank fate.

Childhood

Sinuous strap of leather, slid open
a confused fear of experience
pained by memory fresh in life so near
and buried far beneath welts now aged.

Now it bloomed, a flower so red,
choked in birth, over and over,
and resisting a death, fighting strong
for life that surged within the deep.

Larger it grew, and distance collapsed
upon a pate bare, except that mark
from birth, now bold within an edge
of sharpened means and surety.

Darkening descent of flesh
so forced upon your visage
to thieve the very breath
between your clench of lips.

Oh, a fight for life so long,
fuelled by desperate struggle
and indomitable will to remove
the stinging salt from unhealed wounds.

Yet end it must, so abrupt it fades
from tainted remembrances
poisoned with rapier sharpness
to thrust you from your kin.

Darkness now benign and soft
takes comfort to your feverish heart
to remove his stain and lull
your mind into troubling sleep.

The Dunny Can Man

A species of feces

When I was four, my father sold our house on the hill to pay for a small 400 square foot shop he built on Hastings Street, the main street of Noosa Heads. He and my pregnant mother slept at the back of the shop, in a 100 square foot room walled off in the corner, and I slept in a bunk bed concealed by a curtain behind the counter. The simple kitchen was in a narrow corridor behind a bamboo curtain.

We washed outside using a basin of water, and our toilet was an outhouse, colloquially referred to as a "dunny". This outhouse contained a cubical box with a hole in the top and a wooden lid that had to be kept closed to keep out the flies. On the front of this cubical box was a door to access the interior, and inside was a large metal can with handles.

As there was no sewage system in the small village, the shire council employed men to come during the early morning hours to remove the "night soil" from the all of the outhouses in the town. Once a week, they would carry out this chore by replacing the full can with an empty one. They would then load the full cans onto a truck called a "dunny cart" and drive to a spot where a large pit had been dug in the sand. Here, they would empty the cans into this pit. They hosed out the cans and covered over the fresh, human excrement with a layer of sand. If the can was showing signs of rust or contained small punctures, they would dip the can in hot tar to coat it. This would protect and seal the can.

A man who carried out the work of collecting and dealing with this human waste, was called a "dunny can man".

I grabbed a pole from the ground
and shoved it through the fence.
Now across the narrrow path,
a hurdle I would sense.

Down I ran towards the pole,
and leaped high in the air.
I cleared it well with a young boy's legs,
with plenty of room to spare.

Childhood

Over and over, I did my leap,
the joy of flying high.
My mother called, it was time to eat,
I'd come back by and by.

My belly full, I forgot my quest
and settled with a book.
Night came on and I grew tired,
sleep crept up and me it took.

In early morn, there came a crash,
a curse so loud and clear.
A clatter of cans, and then a thump.
A poor soul hurt, I fear.

When I awoke, I heard the tale
of what had caused the clatter.
The dunny can man had come to grief
and the contents all a splatter.

In the dark, he'd walked the path,
the heavy can he held.
He reached the pole that I had left,
and there it had him felled.

The oath he swore was not for ears
as young as mine had been.
When I was told what I had caused,
I lost my innocent mien.

"It's not my fault", I stated clear.
"I didn't know, I'm sure."
My father spoke with such firm words.
"You'll clean up this manure."

Years went by, and I grew high,
I ran and jumped and creeped.
But never again would I make
a hurdle for me to leap.

The Fight

A hurricane of hurt

My confusion about relationships and violence was too mysterious and traumatic for me to resolve on my own. To cope, I developed a simple system which, while it stood me in good stead over many years, eventually came to limit and even cripple my social ability. My feelings became binary, I either felt good or felt bad. If I felt bad, I did things that would make me feel good. Such a simplistic means of judging the impact of events made it very difficult in later life to understand the feelings and subtle nuances in my relationships with friends, partners and spouses.

I became able to shut out the world during times of high stress; I coped with adults who became aggressive, by automatically perceiving them to be tiny people far away. Additionally, blood would flow into my inner ear region, swelling tissues so that my hearing became highly attenuated. I was learning to survive in this violent world.

There'd been a fight, a scrap of sorts,
between a bully and me.
I ran for home, my own safe fort
where I could be so free.

Inside my house, I looked about
and saw to my dismay,
my mother was there, and some big lout
was standing in my way.

"Why the pout?" my mother had asked.
"And your clothes are dirty and torn."
Before I could speak, the stranger came close.
"I was there when you were born."

He looked me up and and then back down
and saw my bloody knees.
"Wot's this?" he said with a great big frown,
and I felt so ill at ease.

Childhood

I looked at him and then to my mom,
but she said not a single word.
I looked back and went quite dumb,
and this is what I heard.

"Wazza matter, did a cat get yer tongue?"
As he towered so high over me.
He was so big and I so young,
and I felt the need to pee.

My mouth fell open and my eyes shone fear,
I wanted to be with my mom.
But he stood so close and I felt so queer,
I knew not what to be done.

In a flash I cried, my tears spilled out,
my words were close behind.
"He beat me up!" I began to shout,
but quelled from my state of mind.

From far away, I heard him speak,
this supposed uncle of mine.
"Well, we'll fix that, you won't be weak!"
And he laid it on the line.

"Yer gonna learn to be a man,
I'll teach ya how to box."
He grabbed a cushion off the sedan,
and hauled me out in shock.

Against the fence, he tied the cushion,
and pushed me up to it.
"Now punch it, boy, y're on a mission.
G'wan, givet a hit!"

I stood quite still, hearing his jeers,
my heart was pumping fast.
The blood it swelled within my ears,
'till silence reigned at last.

Childhood

"Punch it now, wazza matter with you?
Can't ya take a swing?"
"Yer a coward, without a damn clue.
It's a pillow, a soft little thing."

I gave a weak punch, then burst into tears,
My thin little arms at my side.
I had never done this in all my years,
and could not, though I tried.

"Ahh, wazza point! Ya'll never 'mount
to anythin', I can see.
I'm goin' inside, you sort it out."
With that he took his leave.

I made my way, I know not how,
to my hiding place in the trees.
There I sat for many a long hour,
hugging my bony knees.

I came on home, with my tattered clothes,
the lights were all a-lit.
I sneaked up the stairs, on my tippy-toes,
at the door I was ready to split.

The uncle had gone, my dad had come home,
and dinner was there near my chair.
They said not a word, nor asked where I roamed,
while I ate 'till my plate was bare.

I spoke not a word, nor was asked one as well,
and silently went to bed.
It was a bad day, and not wanting to dwell,
I slept the sleep of the dead.

Bullies Vanquished

Tilting at windmills

I was a pacifist by nature and did not understand why other boys wanted to hurt each other. I was frightened by the aggressive displays of the local bullies and found it impossible to go on the offensive to defend myself, preferring instead to use my fast legs to carry me far away.

On one occasion, I had been bailed up in the corner of a school washroom by a group of four bullies and unable to escape. My fear became so great that I exploded into action. I surprised them, and myself, with lightning speed punches, which left them lying on the concrete floor in a stunned state. They avoided me after that.

In my bed so safe and sound,
I dreamed upon my predicament.
There were some boys that I had found,
whose aggression made me vigilant.

I wished that I had the power
to send them to their bed.
I'd make them tremble and really cower,
like heroes in comics I had read.

I imagined that I had the strength
of a great big tall tree.
I'd hold my arms at full length
and run among them free.

In my mind, I saw them run
and scatter for their lives.
I now would never fear none
and worry on how to survive.

When I awoke, I began to see
that nothing had come about.
The world would still not let me be,
and I was due for a few more clouts.

The Pedal Car

Driving into near oblivion

Walter Vivian Tronson lived near the end of Hastings Street. Earlier in his life, he owned Ringwood Farm, raising chickens and cattle outside of Tewantin, about five kilometres up the Noosa River. The land contained a low-lying and swampy lagoon and, to improve the pastures, he decided to drain it. It was during the Great Depression, when many people were unemployed and were willing to work at anything they could get. He hired up to thirteen men for two dollars a day, and they set about to dig a kilometre-and-a-half long canal, four metres wide and a metre deep. The canal still exists and is called Tronson's Canal.

In his younger days, Walter was a boxer and became the Middle Weight Champion of Queensland. An excerpt from the Toowoomba Chronicle, 8th February 1909, reads:

> JENNINGS AND TRONSON
>
> Boxing contests are evidently fashionable here now, as the Toowoomba Athletic Club is holding another fight at their new stadium at the running grounds. This will be the third fight since its inauguration and will be the best of the lot, as the men are evenly matched, both in weight and science. Jennings, who is a good boxer with a good record, having 44 fights to his credit, winning 40, drawing twice, and losing once on points, and has never been knocked out.
>
> Tronson, a young fighter, with a terrific punch, who defeated Max Pardella a few weeks ago here, will arrive in a few days and should give a good account of himself.
>
> Jennings will spar at the stadium tomorrow (Wednesday) afternoon at 3 o'clock. The public are cordially invited.
>
> Outcome - Walter Tronson won knocking out Jennings in the third round.[1]

---

1 http://writerspen.com.au/bushorchestra/family_logo/life_of/TronsonBiographyWalter.html

Childhood

Walter Tronson was 76 years old at the time of this near collision between his car and me in the pedal car.

One fine day in my town,
my excitement was at its peak.
My friend just got a pedal car,
it was really his for keeps.

I watched him very diligently,
with a lot of boyish jealousy,
as he pedalled hard along the street
and came back breathlessly.

There came a time when he did tire,
and handed me the wheel.
In a flash I was seated down,
it was such a great big deal.

I speared out between parked cars,
the other side I was headed.
There came a scream of tires so loud,
and the impact soon I dreaded.

I was unscathed but continued on,
in spite of a deep voice holler.
Before I reached the other side,
the driver had grabbed my collar.

He picked me up and shook me hard,
then beat me with his fist.
I was so shocked, I knew not who
had pinned my by my wrist.

He dragged me back across the street
and took me to my mom.
His face was red and his eyes popped out,
and my arm was going numb.

Childhood

"I just about killed your son,
here's your little Pete.
You better make sure that he stays home,
and you keep him off the street."

That night, I was quite sore,
as I went off to bed.
I had been punished twice over,
and wished that I was dead.

Confession

Black Box Analysis

My mother had grown up in a Catholic family and one of the conditions of marriage was that my father was to convert from the Church of England to Catholicism. He attend church for a number of years with my mother and my siblings, however he was finding it more and more in conflict with his emerging atheistic philosophy. His last visit to the church came about when he amused my sister and me with a bra that he had fashioned out of a large, white handkerchief. The shock and outrage this action had engendered in my mother must have brought his disdain for the church to a head and he no longer attended services with us.

I continued attending church until I was sixteen as it was considered a compulsory obligation by my mother, however as soon as I left home to go out to work, I rarely found myself inside the walls of a church except for a wedding or funeral service.

Later, I recognized that my scientific thinking style had been well formed quite early in life and I realized that at the age of seven, I had been conducting a classic "Black Box Analysis" of the church's confessional system. I was providing a variety of inputs into an unknown or "black" system and examining the outputs to determine the function or rules that governed this unknown system. Needless to say, my quest to understand this unknown system was fruitless as humans, unlike machines, can be quite chaotic. It foretold a profession later in life as a Systems Analyst.

Out of the confessional I had come,
the priest's command remembered.
I had my penance and then some
for my sins that he had heard.

Three "Our Father's" and five "Hail Mary's"
was what he had ordained.
It puzzled me, for he had varied
from last Sunday, when he proclaimed.

Childhood

This confession thing was just brand new
to a boy of seven years time.
I tried to see, but had no clue
how the punishment fit the crime.

I set about to figure it out,
I had a plan so sure.
Throughout the week, I would sin no doubt,
on Sunday, I would examine the cure.

Months went by, and I came no closer
to a solution to my dilemma.
Was annoying our friendly local grocer
worth two or three "Our Father's"?

And what about the time I decided
to use last week's confession.
It was word for word, and yet he provided
A completely different selection.

The world was such a very strange place,
and God was inconsistent.
But I continued testing, just in case
the solution would present itself, insistent.

Years later, I came to know
my experience had a benefit.
It helped me cope with my sweet beau
Or else I'd end up celibate.

The Kittens

Life undertaken

While we lived in the back of the shop, my mother became pregnant with my brother. Space was now becoming a premium with my baby sister in a cot, sharing the tiny bedroom in which my parents slept. Having accumulated enough funds from the shop, my father bought land from my grandmother on which to build a house. This land was on the side of a steep and narrow road to my grandfather's farm on the side of the hill overlooking the village of Noosa Heads.

My grandfather had sold the farm but retained a part of the land that contained four large mango trees and had the land divided into three lots. My father bought the lot that was farthest from the main street. When the house was completed, we moved to our new but unfinished house.

I was about nine years old when I experienced an event that would have a profound effect on my life. Afterwards, as a young boy, I often had cardboard boxes sheltering injured birds and other animals to allow them to recover from their wounds. Some died despite my care as I had tried hard to atone myself for the blame I felt. I do not understand the perverseness that led my grandmother to expose me to an event that, although a common occurrence, should not have been something that a child need experience.

A sound...a sound I heard
from the shed...a storage shed.
A cry...a little cry,
more cries.

I looked...I sought,
I found...yes, there on the heap
of old grain sacks, they were.
My heart, it felt the warmth.

Childhood

Kittens three, crying to me,
with little mouths, little paws.
Soft, soft fur, ever so soft
as my little hands touched.

Into my shirt, they went.
Oh, so warm, soft and warm.
Moving, kneading...exploring,
my bare skin...tickling.

Head for home, I did not know
what to do...oh, what to do?
The day ending, the sun setting,
through our window...my mom.

"Can I look after them, Mom?
I found them, Mom."
"No...not here, someone else,
Try somewhere else."

Night came on, all the same.
"I'm sorry." "We have a cat."
"No...no...no, not here."
"Try down the road."

Grandma's house...she likes cats.
Kittens three...so warm...so soft,
moving, kneading...breathing,
my bare skin...prickling.

"What do you have?...Yes,
kittens three...I see...I see.
Too many kittens...much too many,
what to do...oh, what to do."

"Come with me...and bring those three."
Down the stairs...underneath,
light turned on, a tub...a laundry tub,
and hands upon the tap.

Childhood

A tub...a tub, a wash tub,
yes, a bath...they must be cleaned.
The water flowed in, higher and higher,
'Till it came near the top.

"Give them me...here into my hands,
hold open that sack...good, good."
"This is right...They have no mom,
don't worry...it's all for the best."

Into the sack they went.
Oh, so warm, soft and warm,
moving, climbing...mewing,
my bare skin...tingling.

What is this?...I do not know,
what to do...oh, what to do.
The sack descending, the water closing.
How long...how long will you hold it?

All those bubbles...those pretty bubbles,
tiny and soft..from mouths so small.
Moving, struggling...gasping,
my bare skin...shaking.

I see the dark...run into the dark!
Run! Run! Run!
Breathing! Breathing hard,
panting...aching...struggling.

Up the stairs...Fast, Faster!
Through the open door...Slam!
It shut...it blocked...no outside.
Breathing! Breathing fast...home.

"Where have you been?
Look at you...now look at you.
Wait...What's wrong,
what happened, tell me...to me."

Childhood

Oh, the scream, the cry...not mine,
burst forth, bubbling between lips.
Breathe! Breathe fast.
What to say...oh, what to say.

Into her blouse I went.
Oh, so warm, soft and warm,
holding, hugging...weeping,
my bare skin...shivering.

A sound...a sound I heard,
from somewhere deep...within a well.
A cry...a little cry,
more cries.

The Tree House

And lead us not into adventure

At our new home, my sister and I would play in mango trees that my grandfather had planted many decades before. They were large and spreading, and as they grew, the older and larger bottom limbs slowly lowered until they were horizontal. This made a perfect platform upon which to build tree houses.

After our house was built, the left-over construction wood was piled on "The Wood Heap". We used this old material in combination with various wooden fruit boxes, which we dismantled and de-nailed to use for the frame and walls of our tree houses. My grandmother had some scraps of carpet she had saved, which she gave us to line the floor.

C'mon Mom!
Come an' see what we have done!
We've built a tree house,
it's so much fun.

Oh, I don't know.
Your dear Grandma
needs her lunch
or she will crow.

Oh, c'mon now,
don't be a sow.
It won't take long,
you'll be back afore the hour.

Oh, you kids,
let me check these ribs,
And if they're okay,
well…you best not be telling a fib.

Truly, we built it today,
me an' Michelle, hey.
We made it strong,
it's really okay.

Childhood

Alright love,
please reach above
for my coat.
You're such a dove.

Follow us
and please don't cuss.
It's in the big mango
down by the old bus.

That's so far,
should we go by car?
I don't want to be long
'cause I left the door ajar.

You can see it from here,
it's very clear
Up on that branch,
there's nothing to fear.

It looks so good!
I didn't think you could
You build this yourself?
My! And it has a hood.

No, that's the porch.
Here, I'll shine the torch.
Grab hold of the ladder,
it won't scorch.

Climb up there?
My! I don't think I dare.
What if I slip,
and my dress I tear?

Oh, Mom don't be a dunce!
When you've done it once,
you'll be proud of what we did,
and you can even share our lunch.

Childhood

I shouldn't do this.
Quick, give me a kiss
and I'll try my best
not to puff and hiss.

Mom! Good on you!
You're climbing strong and true.
You're at the top
and not even blue.

Ooooh! I don't know,
It's moving so.
Lovely house, but put back that ladder,
I want to go!

You haven't seen it yet,
just look at the carpet.
Grandma gave us that,
you can sleep on it, I bet.

Oh no, it's way to small
and I'm just too tall
Now kids, put back the ladder,
I'm so scared, I'll start to bawl.

Oh mom, you're such a wimp,
Michelle can climb like a imp.
Okay, here's the ladder,
c'mon down, pretend you're a chimp.

Oh, thank God I'm on the ground, phew!
That was quite an adventure, it's true.
You know, I love you so much that
your old mom will do anything for you.

Yeah mom, that's what we thought.
Now come with us, you aught
to try our raft, it's in the river.
We built it! It's not bought!

Old Men in the Shadows

A war to end all peace

My great-grandfather, Ernest George Greber, fought in World War I and was awarded the Military medal for outstanding bravery on August 8, 1918. The award citation states:

> ...Pte Ernest George Greber (number 4877), 31st Battalion, 13th reinforcement, enlisted on 30th August 1916 was awarded the Military Medal in 1918 for outstanding bravery on 8th august 1918 during an attack on 31st battalion from Warfusee-Abancourt. This man did wonderful work in stretcher bearing showing an absolute disregard for his personal safety. He not only carried in his own men but also many of the 2nd Australian Division which had passed our lines. He was absolutely indefatigable and continued work until all the wounded had been cleared setting a wonderful example of courage and endurance to his comrades.

As a young man, I was curious about war, and from the stories my mother and father had told, I knew that my ancestors and relatives had fought in both world wars. I sensed the horror of war from the reactions my relatives displayed when pressed to describe their experiences.

Old men in shadows of the night,
seen, but never heard.
The story of their life and fight
for us, a peace not stirred.

From the clamour of youth now spent,
in battles with mud and fence,
their nascent fear still makes them tense,
many a long time hence.

"Show us your bullet wound, grandpa,
and your medal bright."
Eyes cast up from the hand held card,
did we ask him right?

Childhood

*Did they ask too much of me that day,
of this here broken man.
But my cobber's life was held in sway,
lying hurt in no-man's land.*

*Crawling under broken strands
of wire so barbed to hurt,
I took great care with my hands,
so my arms it would not girt.*

"You got it in the war, grandpa?"
Stained finger reach his lips,
where cigar stub sat in his craw,
while smoke curled up in strips.

*The journey to my mate was long,
I had to keep my pluck.
Behind my back, the river Somme,
half buried in the muck.*

*Quick, quick, now move so fast
in this poor land out here.
Breathing smoke, a shell shocked blast
that pressed against my ear.*

"C'mon, grandpa," we gathered round.
"Show us your wounded leg."
He took his stub and pushed it down,
and pressed it like a peg.

The curl of smoke broke off quite cold,
banished from our scent.
In the tray, the cigar it rolled,
then stopped as a bullet spent.

*I found him quick, thank God for that,
I found him in the dark.
We should get on, no time to chat,
I must be on my mark.*

Childhood

He is quite heavy and worse for wear,
do I really have the might?
High above, a bright white flare
brought the filthy mud to light.

"Grandpa?" we said and tugged his sleeve,
as we watched him reach down low.
With gnarled fingers on tired wool weave
his leg began to show.

The light it caught us in the field,
and showed them where we were.
"C'mon mate, I'm your shield,
We'll get you cross this spur."

An eagle eye, one of youth,
saw those moving three.
A finger squeezed the trigger smooth,
and set that bullet free.

We stared so hard at muscle torn,
a scar that hollowed calf.
"Had the bullet went through and gone?
You're missing nearly half."

I felt the heat, but not the pain,
and heard my voice just grunt.
I had been shot, to my bane,
way out beyond the front.

I had no care, I was as good as dead,
it mattered not at all.
"Let's go, mate, I'll stand in your stead,
we gotta get up this wall."

With steely eye, I began to climb
to home across the mud.
In decaying light, the flesh and grime
had mingled with my blood.

Childhood

"You were so brave," we began to boast.
"Did you have much blood?"
He stared across at unseen ghosts,
and his tears began to flood.

With rheumy eyes, a little wet,
he shook his head so slow.
But no words came and he began to fret,
his pain began to show.

*The wire it cut like a sharpened knife,
and heavy was his weight.
The mud it sucked and pulled at life,
and demanded that we wait.*

*In a deep wide hole, we sat on dirt,
but dared not take a rest.
My fingers cramped, and my leg it hurt.
Oh, the agony of my quest.*

"You got a medal, you saved some bloke.
Is that how you got shot?"
We followed him to a box of oak,
that was fastened by a knot.

*Closer came the looming berm,
where there would spell our fates.
I saw the barrels poke and squirm.
"Don't shoot, we are your mates!"*

"Do you wear it?" we had to shout,
for we were so enthralled.
"Once a year I take it out,
Armistice Day it's called."

Once again we coaxed and tried.
"How come you were so brave?"
His head he shook from side to side,
and dismissed us with a wave.

Puberty

First Kiss

Experience in matters of the heart and flesh

I met some distant relatives one day, one of them a girl who was a second or third cousin my age. Although we were both thirteen years old at the time, she had vastly more experience than I did in matters of the heart (and flesh). I was no match for her.

It was my first emotional experience with a female and, as it was so new to me, my reaction was close to being in shock. Afterwards, I was convinced it had all been a dream.

One nice day, they came to stay,
some relatives I was told.
There was a girl, about my age,
a cousin and how she strolled.

She caught my eye and I did spy
a twinkle that stirred my blood.
Her lips creased up into a smile,
and my heart began to thud.

We walked the beach, and she did teach
me things I did not know.
Her hand caught mine in her grasp,
and my nerves began to show.

We sat a while, she showed her guile,
and teased me with her voice.
I was confused, I must admit.
I did not have much choice.

Puberty

She spoke so soft, and touched me oft,
I came close to hear her speak.
"Have you kissed a girl," I heard her say,
and my knees went very weak.

I stammered much, from her touch,
I had no words that day.
"I..well…ahhh,"
was all I heard me say.

She took my face in an embrace,
and brought her lips to mine.
I sat transfixed, my brain a whirl,
as a shiver ran down my spine.

I did not know, for time was slow,
how long we were enjoined.
It seemed an age, in another world,
and I felt a stirring in my loin.

A dream, I thought. I knew I aught
to take some time to think.
I'd never felt this way before,
and my face was turning pink.

She drew away, and began to say
some words I did not hear.
I looked at her with dreamy eyes,
afraid she'd disappear.

She gave a laugh, and grasped her scarf.
"Let's go", she said to me.
"We must go back, it's getting late,
I think it's time for tea."

I'll not forget, you can bet,
that lovely day in June.
I know I kissed, but that I missed,
all I did was swoon.

Last Beating

Mother and son in the bathroom of pain

Children normalize abuse to the point where they often have no awareness of the wrongness of it all. Sometimes, the shock of an anticipated trauma can provide the necessary impetus to dramatically change one's maturity. This is one such moment.

Where is he? He should be here,
and dinner is almost ready.
He's late, he's very late,
I'm tense and need to be steady.

A bird, A bird, I found a bird,
the wing, it looks so bent.
The eyes, so black, so small,
look at me from heaven sent.

It's dark outside, so very dark,
I remember the great big chest.
I was trapped, I could not leave,
my cousin, on the lid he pressed.

In my arms, I carried it gently,
its feathers so soft and smooth.
A home for it, I hoped to find,
its trauma I wished to sooth.

The dinner ready, the family called,
all save one was sat.
My face a-fire and skin all taut,
oh where, oh where is he at!

Through the town, I walked and walked,
looking to find some one.
My little bird, so very quiet now,
was looking completely stunned.

Puberty

He must be near, he's got to be near,
I cannot have him gone.
Am I to blame, and did I fail,
a mother to my first-born son.

Under the streetlight, my poor bird
lay still, its heart had stopped.
I turned it over with gentle care,
but its little head just dropped.

I must find him, where's my coat?
Out in the dark I strode.
I called and called, my voice now hoarse,
echoing down the road.

In the sand, I dug a hole,
and placed its feathered shape.
So perfect, yet without the spark,
from Death, it did not escape.

I feel the rage, my impotence raw,
I had to take some action.
Back to the house, I went reluctant,
to eat my meal in distraction.

The moonlit mound revealed a tale
that only I could read.
I straightened up and headed home,
and lateness gave me speed.

I can't take it, I must stand up,
my heart it beat so hard.
Fists are clenched, I break my cup,
a finger cut from shard.

I see the lights all aglow,
home it made me feel.
Through the door, I quickly flowed
into warmth and light and meal.

Puberty

He's here, he's here!
I feel my rage within.
My self control now disappears,
and I am my evil twin.

Her eyes burn dark and very deep,
and face becomes a mask.
That look I know, my fear it leaps,
and I know what soon she'll ask.

"All this night, where have you been!"
I hear my voice so strange.
My devilled twin could be so mean,
as I felt my self to change.

"A bird! A bird! I found a bird!"
I cried in deep despair.
"I gave it help, but it had not stirred,
in spite of all my prayers."

I felt the stick with my grasp,
a broken piece of broom.
I yelled so loud, my voice a rasp,
as I dragged him to the room.

A change had come from somewhere strange,
I had never known this calm.
In all the times of violent exchange,
there never was a balm.

With every blow I rained on him,
I told him of his sin.
I beat him hard from limb to limb,
which made a fearful din.

From far away, I looked with truth,
at the boy that I once was.
And in his place, stood a youth
with a heart of noble cause.

Puberty

Through rage I knew, there was a wrong,
he did not squirm and scream.
I saw him stand so very strong,
and saw his self-esteem.

I did not feel the stick so hard,
nor the bruise and welts so many.
For steady as a palace guard,
I stood my ground as any.

Through my craze, I saw my ill,
and knew that I was taken.
He had broken me of all my will.
and had left me so forsaken.

I watched the stick slip from her hand,
to clatter on the floor.
I knew that this was not her plan,
for I had robbed her of her chore.

With guilt and shame and confusion plain,
I left him in his world.
With dragging steps in so much pain,
I felt my spirit whirl.

I was transformed, and knew I'd won,
but at such a terrible loss.
Nevermore would we have fun,
but she not be my boss.

At the table, I sat so stunned,
a feeling I did not know.
I missed the bond, now I was shunned,
it added to my woe.

A day had passed, and life moved fast,
it carried on as before.
Yet my life was fresh, a new die cast,
with my soul uplifted and a-soar.

I Walk the Line

Upon a painted world

I was thirteen when I obtained my first job outside my town with a surveyor laying out a new multi-lane highway. The road was to pass though tens of kilometres of virgin rain forest to the east of the town of Caboolture. The survey crew had used axes and brush hooks to hack a narrow and straight corridor through which to sight the theodolite, and lay out the centre line of the new motorway. To make the centre line more visible, white paint was used to mark protruding logs, branches and any obstruction along the line.

A lad I was, when I got some work,
my mom and friend did chat.
"Ask your man, I know it's a perk."
"He'll take your boy, and that's just that!"

My mom was pleased, for she had feared
I would become a lout.
She wanted me to have a career,
with my future not in doubt.

School was done, and I was free
to surf and swim…but wait,
I have to work, my mom had said,
stunned by the hand of fate.

That first day, with leaden feet,
down the road I was told.
My new boss, a man I feared,
stood grimly, looking cold.

I entered the truck, what could I do?
We drove for such a long time,
Till at last we reached his crew,
all standing in their prime.

Puberty

One big man, held a pot,
large and all a-drip.
"Look over there, beyond that lot
At the pickets? Now take a grip."

"Here's ya can, and here's ya brush!"
"What?" I spoke so soft.
"Ya paint a line, there is no rush.
Grab it, you best be off."

"But what do I paint?" I felt so dense.
"It's simple," he told me.
"Every chopped down tree and a fence,
paint a line where the road's gonna be."

"What road?" for I had no gist.
"We're buildin' a road," he teased.
Reaching out his sun burnt fist,
I felt my thin arm squeezed.

"Stand behind and look so straight,
at the stake that I depict.
See that fence, the log and gate
in line with this sharp stick?"

I nodded dumbly, for I could see,
and walked towards the fence.
The brush was full and paint sprayed free.
"Ya got it!" he called from whence.

All alone, I walked the line,
cross logs that showed the mark.
I dressed them with my virgin brine
as I climbed their hardened bark.

Deep in forest, where liana vines
curled their way in roves.
With heavening weight of my white lines,
from a brush that swung and wove.

Puberty

Through a swamp, I held a-high
my pot of heavy weight.
It pressed itself against my thigh,
my white arm holding freight.

Sun rose high, and heat grew bright
upon my sweaty toil.
Brushed fingers stuck from titanium white
and drying linseed oil.

Still that line went on, I vowed,
and forever to the west.
I swayed and stumbled over boughs,
driven forward on my quest.

Rain forest gloom made a veil
from the brilliance of my toil,
as the lowering sun and lightened pail,
buoyed my spirits royal.

Ahead, I spied a clearing bright,
with fence and stump a-kneel.
I set my sights and ran a-sprite,
to daub them with my zeal.

Into the open, I burst right through
and looked about abrupt.
I once again had joined the crew,
work paused in interrupt.

"What the heck!" I heard a yell,
and swivelled on the earth.
There stood my boss, his chest a-swell
and shaking in his mirth.

"You're in the back, that's my two cents,
you're not with us, that's fine!
Did ya think you was a fence
a-standing on the line?"

Puberty

I gave a look at the brute,
he smiled from head to toe.
"Look at y'self, ya stupid galoot,
you're covered in the snow."

A brush in hand and can on sleeve,
I eyed myself in fright.
In reddening sun and cooling eve,
I stood in vestments white.

Riding My Tanka Bike

Life on the road

I have been a cyclist all of my life, reveling in the sheer pleasure of moving fast along a road. What better way to express my exuberance than by using this form of poetry.

On the road again,
and speeding my bike along.
Wind through my long hair,
with tires a-humming loudly,
as we speed down the steep hill.

At the very bottom,
I straighten up and pedal
fast along the road,
to reach shelter in a shed,
before the thunderstorm strikes.

Now the path so fresh,
glistens with wet from the rain.
Spray from my black wheel,
to shiver my wet cold legs,
and muddy my red bike shoes.

Ahead, I see home,
and speed my way towards it.
The sun bakes my back
and warms my skin and muscles.
Great ride on my Tanka bike!

Adolescence

Home for Men

Homelessness and salvation

When I finished with high school, I went surfing every day. My father wanted me to get a job and leave home, so he came up with a plan to make it happen. He decided that as there were few real jobs in Noosa Heads, a tourist town, I was to find work in Brisbane. He told me that I could stay at the Salvation Army Home for Men on Stanley Street in South Brisbane for free until I got a job.

What he did not tell me, was that in using the Home for Men as my residential address when applying for work, would virtually guarantee that no one would employ me. It was the place of last refuge for alcoholics.

"You must leave, you cannot stay."
"You're too old to stay at home."
I was told, I'd be okay,
provided I did not roam.

I had ten dollars, enough he said
to get me on my feet.
There's a place where you'll be fed,
and there'll be much to eat.

The city you'll go, a day away,
and here is the address written.
You'll catch the bus without delay,
and find a seat to sit in.

Adolescence

The journey long, but I arrived
in Brisbane at the station.
I followed the map, my dad contrived,
and found my destination.

I was young, and all alone,
and fearful as could be.
I reached a wall made of stone,
and a door that needed a key.

A crowd of men began to arrive,
with clothes all tattered and torn.
For them a home, for me a dive,
a life I had not borne.

As we waited, twilight came,
and I huddled against the chill.
Some men were sick, it smelt so bad,
and the gutter began to fill.

At last she came, a woman dressed
in uniform of military attire.
There was a badge, upon her breast,
in colours of bright red fire.

The Salvation Army it was written
in letters so white and clear.
In her hand, clothed in a mitten,
A key I saw appear.

She opened the door, and led us through
to a courtyard of brick and stone.
We would be fed, and my hunger grew,
but first we had to be shown.

We all were sinners, she was frank,
and we had to make amends.
Before we ate, we'd give our thanks
to the god that was our friend.

Adolescence

Soon more arrived of her ilk
to join us in their song.
The night progressed, and I wanted milk,
my hunger was very strong.

Song after song we belted out,
and I thought I'd never eat.
The promised food, I began to doubt,
and my stomach began to bleat.

At last we filed into a room,
the largest I had ever seen.
And what I saw was like a tomb,
with tables and chairs all clean.

We sat to eat, but first came grace,
read by a man in black.
As he spoke, I saw his face
spy me, and then draw back.

Into the room, carrying a pot,
bigger than I'd ever seen,
two men in white, stained with blots,
followed by another tureen.

The bowls came next, then some ladles,
and into the pots they went.
I grabbed the spoon from the table,
and over my bowl I bent.

The soup was thin, but all the same
I ate it with some bread.
And after the meal, another man came
to lead us to our bed.

Row upon row, our cots and gunny
filled that great big dorm.
Under my pillow, I placed by money,
and hoped it'd be there by morn.

Adolescence

Before I slept, the man who spoke,
came over to my side.
"You shouldn't be here with these poor folk.
You're much too young!" he cried.

When I awoke, we were fed
a gruel that was okay.
I ate it with some bread,
and hot tea from the tray.

I left that place with a letter,
to help me earn a wage.
There was home that would be better,
and more suited to my age.

The next few weeks, I did live
at a home for orphaned boys.
My life was better, but I would give
anything to leave that noise.

I got a job, and I was blessed,
but it was far away.
I had to leave and head northwest,
a tale for another day.

Desolation

Melting pot of powerful influences

Rachael Carson was a strong influence in my youth, and this poem was encouraged by her writings. Perhaps, in my nascent environmental experience, I was anticipating climate change and sea level rise.

I was surprised that I had personified nature as masculine. I have no memory of that decision, as I was not in control of the words which poured out of me, prodded by a powerful muse.

The poem also contains interesting elements of Chapter 11 of H. G. Wells, *The Time Machine* and was also inspired by the poem *Ozymandias* by Percy Bysshe Shelley:

> I met a traveller from an antique land
> Who said: "Two vast and trunkless legs of stone
> Stand in the desert. Near them, on the sand
> Half sunk, a shattered visage lies, whose frown
> And wrinkled lip, and sneer of cold command
> Tell that its sculptor well those passions read
> Which yet survive, stamped on these lifeless things
> The hand that mocked them and the heart that fed:
> And on the pedestal these words appear:
> "My name is Ozymandias, king of kings:
> Look on my works, ye Mighty, and despair!"
> Nothing beside remains. Round the decay
> Of that colossal wreck, boundless and bare
> The lone and level sands stretch far away.

Grinding, seething, clawing, green waves
topped by furious foam,
whipped by strengthening wind,
tearing apart buoyant life,
thrusting upon hard, harsh encrusted rocks.

Nothing remains,
except bleached bones rejected by a conqueror.

Adolescence

Salt spray kills sand-strangled trees,
spider grass driven into sand-blasted hell.
A lone crab staggers, falls,
and disappears into an avalanche of waste.

Rotting carcass dragged across barnacles,
a mushroom of green water surges and sweeps
the very shell of the foundation.
Muffled explosion, wall of water rises to claim the air.

Skeletal dwelling shakes, sways in wind
too strong to house all but blown plastic, glass,
and the detritus of some ancient civil life,
to show little of their efforts.

They claimed all to claim none, while life found its way
to spit its power into puny faces, long gone,
that encroached on his rights.
Someday, maybe some day, one day...maybe...

Aftermath

First love at sight

I was eighteen, living in a hostel in Bulimba, Brisbane, and had met a woman of my same age with whom I fell into love. She went south to Sydney, Australia for a two week vacation. One evening while she was away, I was hanging out with a group of my friends, listening to some music, when my Muse took me into her confidence.

Two of us, connected, unconnected,
night infused room with smoky lamps,
soft pads absorbing bony limbs.

Sound, powerful, full, with chest vibrating nuance,
symphonic emotion of drum, strings and organs
of my mind, locked across the ages, across the distance.

Desire and pain reach out, and clasp my heart
of longing, to touch, brush, stroke hair, long from eyes,
from face, ever inquisitive of the newness of lips.

Memories to give, to take, to seek, to understand
beauty of love, of self, of unknown fear and concern.
Tears from my mind, weep across pathways slow.

I send my touch, my feelings, eclectic in their youth,
esoteric in my caution of past errors of ill thought effusion,
bubbling through a waterfall of sense.

Calm intrigue intoxicates the ethereal beginnings of a love,
new, lost, supplanted by space, not time. Though of that,
I have much to give, to share, to wrap in a robe of desire.

I drift along the currents of passionate anguish,
flowing down the widening stream of conscious stirrings,
feeling warmth spreading outward from my core.

Adolescence

You breathed life and snapped those tightening bonds
that squeezed the imposition of my heart, facing a trial
of meaningless life, a habit I had clothed myself.

I love you for your stolen acceptance, opening my view
of love lost, missed, taken, and propelled from the past
of times gone, to times of what might be.

Older and younger,
existing in a frozen lock of shaggy membrance
that swims from ear to ear.

Music building to a heart pounding crescendo
of reminiscence with glazed eyes,
tightening throat and solitude.

Funnel

Directing my mind's flow and bottling it for posterity

This describes the sensation I experienced when my Muse invaded my mind and directed me to write its words.

Streaming into a wide red funnel that surges
its power and fullness sweet to capture my
passion nascent and effervescing brain.
I go where it takes me, weaving and
twisting deep into an amusing wall
of tantalizing concern and zeal.
I go where it takes my soul
to weep my passion dry
and draw myself into
infinite darkness, a
void I share with
other long lost
souls of muse
with crooked
beginnings,
sketchless
longings
and loss.
A path
before
shows
ways
I yet
must
walk

Beach of Belonging

Sleeping in the sand of silent soliloquies

Home was a place that I yearned for, yet home was also an unwelcome place. I was an apprentice fitter and turner, working and living in Brisbane during the week, and riding the four hour, 160 kilometres journey, on my 100 cc Suzuki motorcycle, from Brisbane to Noosa Heads, on a Friday after work. Instead of going to my parent's house, I preferred to ride the sandy track from Sunshine beach, into Noosa National Park, and to Alexandria Bay to sleep for the night.

On the beach, all alone, I sit.
Sand, soft white sand, caresses,
and wind ruffles my hair
with the sound of sea, crashing and churning.

All alone, how I like it, thinking,
just thinking, of things with soft thoughts.

I know this beach, it is strong in my mind.
Born to be on it, I live here,
its two walls astride me, its dunes enclose me.

Hands through sand, cool, quiet sand, so sparce.
Beach, bleak, and barren, buttress walls and surging seas.

And my thoughts.

My movements slow, time is gone, and beauty creates me.

Sun behind dunes,
and strengthening wind greys seas into a fury of calm.
Love from the sea to form my blood with pride and life.

Slowly I rise,
and sift myself through the sand, to climb into the dunes.

Adolescence

Among dune grass I sit,
a little creek gurgling and bubbling
through rocks beside.
Clean, clear, cool water to give me life.

Stars shining now in a grey sky upon a grey beach.
Ghost crabs scuttle out and about
to befriend me, and teach me
to bury in the cool sand to sleep.

The sand and me.

Morning sun, a loud crump,
and a long steady slide of sound from breaking wave.
Sandy hair is gently tossed,
while warm light surges into cold bones.

Calls of unseen birds.

Soft swells envelop me, sand comforts me,
rocks support me,
and I live on the land that fathers me.

Island of Sand

Playful passion in a silence of sand

I had been working with a theatre troupe that had a run of a play written by the Australian playwright, Mona Brand, called *On Stage Vietnam*. I was the lighting operator who worked one of the spotlights, and a powerful carbon arc machine installed in the theatre. Later, I was an extra, dressed as an Australian soldier conscripted to Vietnam.

After the last night of production, the troupe celebrated at a party held in the director's home. The party was gate-crashed by a motor-cycle gang of rough and coarse individuals, who proceeded to intimidate and harass the troupe members. The director, an astute individual, slowly circulated among us, whispering instructions for us to act boring and behave enigmatically towards our unwelcome guests. After we were prepped, he replaced the Led Zeppelin LP that was currently playing on the record player, with Igor Stravinsky's Violin Concerto in D. After a few minutes, the bikers started grumbling about not having any fun and organically decided to leave.

The director had arranged for us to go camping on Fraser Island, a 120 kilometre long sand island about 200 kilometres north of Brisbane, over the four day Easter break. On the evening before Good Friday, we drove through the night to catch the ferry from River Heads to Kingfisher Bay.

Once on Fraser Island, an old, six-wheel-drive, World-War-II, Studebaker army truck transported us across to the eastern side. Climbing over the sand dunes to reach the ocean swells crashing on the 120 kilometre long yellow sand beach, the troupe often had to leap out of the truck to push the vehicle through the soft, shifting, dune sand.

We camped by Eli Creek, just south of the wreck of the Maheno, a ship that had been driven onto the beach while under tow on July 7, 1935. The heavily-rusted, steel ship remains on the shoreline, easily accessible at low tide. A little further north of Eli Creek, lay Lake Wabby, slowly being filled in by the encroaching wind-blown sand dunes.

Mining companies started mining the beach and sand dunes for rutile (Titanium dioxide) needed for rocket exhausts for Inter

Adolescence

Continental Ballistic Missiles and for the NASA space program. Once the very heavy, black, rutile sand was removed from among the light, yellow, silica sand, heavy seas from seasonal cyclones easily eroded the beach. A large volume of sand and vegetation was lost from the high dunes that backed the beach. The rutile had acted as a heavy weight to prevent severe erosion of the much lighter sand.

The troupe, comprising mostly late teens and young adults, spent three nights and days playing guitar, discussing politics and coming up with solutions for the world's problems. It was an inspiring time for me. I also experienced unrequited love for one of the female members of the troupe, an event that was occurring much too frequently for my confused hormones.

A piece of iron protrudes from sand,
rusted, wrecked, wrought iron
flakes blown by wind, fall upon sand,
driving sand, covered in moments, reshaping.

Over the dune, in a fast-filling, sand valley,
remains a stand of stunted, lightning-struck wood.
No bark, white wood, rotten heart, glazed base.
Shifting, sliding, showering, maze of dunes.

Island, island of life, life abound, life around.
Core of forest, forest of rain and vines, life buttressed.
Balanced by time and eternal existence, now mortal,
natures scales so set off by man's offset.

Men, machines and mendacious meddling,
tearing, torturing, tormented territory of titanium.
Piece by piece, load by load and a deadened heart
no longer fit and fluid, to bend and sway in time.

People advancing, destruction trailing, at their wake.
Now stopped, or almost so, to bring their retreat
over time-frozen plains of wintering despair and turmoil.
What end to our mistakes, errors in waiting?

Adolescence

Forever, a long time, beyond generations of fools,
moronic rule, negligent volition of malicious rationality.
Ironic freedom of thought, purpose, palpable avarice,
driving wisdom to submissive immorality.

A time ahead, so far, too long to call
across reaches of passionate belief and comforted rest,
needed by all in union of life before peace.
And yet another island dies.

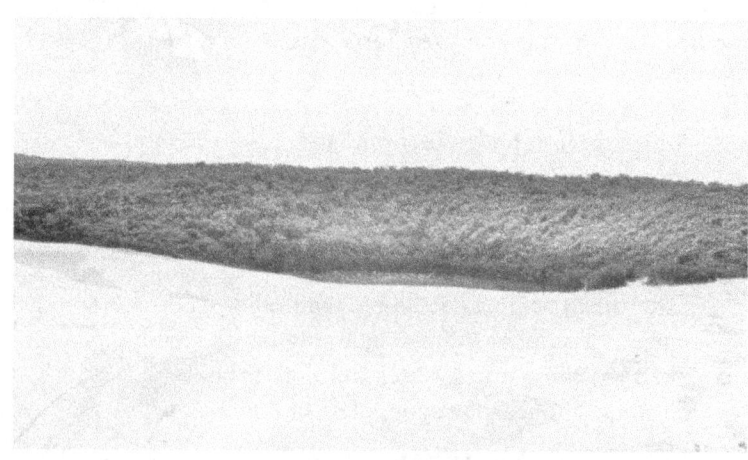

Adulthood

Conscription

A dread of irreparable damage of soul

Australia had various periods of conscription over its history, particularly during World War I, World War II, and the Korean War. In 1964, the Australian government introduced conscription again to support the United States of America in Vietnam. Australia was a signatory to the ANZUS Treaty (Australia, New Zealand and United States Security Treaty). Should one treaty-member country be threatened with aggression by a foreign power, the other countries were committed to come to its aid. As the United States was threatened by Vietnam, Australia and New Zealand sent its troops into the killing fields of South Vietnam to aid the United States.

I was approaching my twentieth birthday and, at which time, I would have to register for conscription or face a long jail term. I could avoid jail if I could prove in court that I had a strong moral objection to all wars, and if I was successful, I would be legalized as a pacifist. This was a virtually impossible task for a young man, and it rarely occurred, as the rate of success was very low.

When I registered, I protested the war by documenting my moral objections in any marginal white space I could find on the registration form. At some interval after my registration form had been filed and tabulated, birth dates were drawn in a lottery system. Fortunately for me, my birth date was not chosen. I thanked my mother for having given birth to me on the day that she did. Had I been born a day earlier or a day later, I might now be fertilizing the jungles of South Vietnam.

I see blue in a red room, where screams of agony,
love and hate, in rapid collapse of any remaining guise.

Adulthood

God! What can she do? Only me,
the paralytic, sucked dry and powerless.

Play, ye piper! Play your tune, play for your master
who pays your wages of sinful reminiscence.

Hate! Hate! Mutilate! Twist and warp your brain.

Don't touch me! I am holy and remain with the spirit given
by the peace of words, not the words of war.

Hate! Hate! Why? Why me?

And the judge sneered.

Jungle of Thoughts

Waring ideas in the green canopy of life

When I thought about the madness of war, I was often assailed by a cacophony of imagery that would make no sense, except for one powerful image that dominated my consciousness.

Jab—Hit—Bash—Wipe—Press—Jerk—Quiver—

How gibberish can you be?
"No more I pray—"
"Praying? Who's he?"
"Don't—"

The little boy sat in the gutter
where the blood of his father ran
and did not understand.
How could he?

Insanity of the sane watching a clarity of monstrous idiocy
How could he understand a demand to be nothing.

"Give me help—"
"Why?"
"What for?"
"I don't get it—do you?"

Spasms—Chasms—

Night in Life

A flow of feeling

A young girl from Sydney ran away from home and hitch-hiked north to the warmth of Queensland. She reached Noosa Heads and was dead broke when she inadvertently met my mother. She begged my mother for a job and became a live-in housekeeper and baby sitter for my eleven year old brother and seven year old younger sister. A few days later, I rode my motorcycle up the coast to see my parents for the weekend, and met her for the first time.

I offered to show her the National Park, and we arranged to take a picnic lunch and walk to Hell's Gates, the bold, steep, eighty-foot high rock buttress that bordered the north end of Alexandria Bay. I encouraged her to climb down the cliff and on one steep section, I was luckily below her when she slipped and fell. Fortunately, I caught her before she plummeted down to the ocean, though she sustained superficial abrasions and cuts on her arms, legs, and feet. As she was walking with pain, I carried her on my back the two kilometres to my parents home, where my mother dressed her wounds.

Later that evening, we went for a walk along the main beach in Lagoona Bay. Near the lifesaver's clubhouse, we sat on the cool soft sand and passionately expressed our love for each other. I was on fire.

> Tension, fear, anxiety. Lost hope.
> I went to bed. I slept.
>
> Cool breeze, the covers slid down.
> Warmth, tension, drifting consciousness,
> soft and sweet.
>
> Tension.
>
> Warm and spice, cool and soft.
> Clutch, brush, drawing closer. Ragged breath.
>
> Feelings drawn out. Passion, explosion.

Adulthood

Action, body, movement. Tasting.

Closer, clutching, whispering, rhythm, sound.

Tension.

Rising, falling, climbing.

Ecstasy.

Urging, calling, mumbled words pouring.
Moving, ever moving.

More.

Breath exhaled, head droops, collapses.
Muscles jelly, folding bodies.

Slow breathing, body sigh, dim senses.

Sleep.

The Charge

Right is might

I went with my friends to demonstrate against Apartheid in front of the Tower Mill motel, where the South African Springbok rugby football team was staying. At some point during the evening, the police were becoming difficult to control and discipline broke down as they charged into the crowd of demonstrators.

> The Springbok rugby team arrived in Brisbane the next day on Thursday 22nd July, 1971. That evening, approximately 300 demonstrators assembled outside the Tower Mill motel on Wickham Terrace where the Springbok's were being accommodated. The protest was relatively small in size as most sports-lovers stayed away from the Tower Mill demonstrations believing the convenient lie about mixing politics and sport. The demonstrators faced about the same number of police lined up in front of the Tower Mill motel. Police in plain clothes mingled with the demonstrators and acted as agents provocateurs.
>
> Without warning, the line of uniformed police marched forward. The demonstrators were forced down the steep, poorly-lit hill in Wickham Park behind them. The police followed attacking with fists, batons and boots under the cloak of darkness. Some protesters escaped by jumping down an eight metre high embankment into the busy traffic of Albert Street below. Others were simply thrown over this cliff.[2]

I was able to avoid being beaten, and safely reached the square outside the City Hall. A large crowd of angry demonstrators was forming, and an agent provocateur was trying to incite them to burn down a police station. When that failed to incite the crowd, he encouraged them to occupy City Hall, which was being used to present a classical music concert at the time. I argued vociferously with this agent provocateur, deflected his power until the crowd slowly dissipated.

---

2 http://www.radicaltimes.info/PDF/SpringbokDemos.pdf

Adulthood

Girl screams from pounding fists
that smashed her breasts into bruised recognition,
distorted face unrecognizable.
Mouth agape, pours out a cry
to makes trees shudder.

Blood pours from eye of running man,
holding his cracked brain in hands
covered with blood from his mouth, choking him.
No humans, many animals. No control.

Hysterical girl stays in the gutter.
Crowd gathers, tensions high, voices loud.
No reason, no sense, no duty, responsibility lost
among the soffing of palms,
swaying in the night-lit square.

Evil direction, confused compliance.
Voice raised in devious passion,
rebuttal lifted with determined derision,
dissipation in anticipation.

***

Here in bed, all is quiet.
Slow wind, rustling gums beyond a dark window.
Gentle calling of magpie.

Sun through window, withdraws broken,
forced back by swinging branches.
Quiet.

Hours before, light of life came through trees,
giving way to a tumult of people.
Beauty, love, passion.

Tricked, crushed, withdrawn, broken, bashed
through the swinging branches.
All is quiet. What next?

Night with the Gypsies

Night moth flying into the heat of Flamenco

As a cadet surveyor working for the Main Roads Department in Queensland, we were conducting a survey near the town of Woodford, about thirty kilometres north-west of Caboolture. I was playing some folk music on my guitar one evening, when a new chain-man, who had joined our gang, was brought into the hut for introductions. He found a spare bunk, tossed his duffel bag on it and sauntered over to me.

"Do you mind if I play your guitar for a bit?" he asked me.

"No worries," I replied.

He picked up the guitar and started to play Malagueña. I had never heard Flamenco before, and I instantly realized that this was the music I wanted to play. I would devote my life to playing it. I begged him to teach me; he immediately sat down beside me, and showed me enough to get me started.

He had a flamboyant personality, which fitted his passionate guitar playing. Years before, he had gotten into a fight in a pub, lost part of his little finger on his left hand, and from being kicked in the stomach, also had a colostomy.

He borrowed my guitar one night, and went into town to woo a woman on whom he had cast his devilish eye. The next day, he described in embarrassing detail to me, how he had seduced her. I could understand it, as the music had seduced me. I was in love with it.

Unfortunately, he did not stay with us for long, as his passionate personality ran afoul of the surveyor in charge of the gang. He was fired.

Later, I moved to Brisbane and sought out the Flamenco guitarists playing in the city cafés to teach me. I received good training, but was over-charged by one guitarist who asked me $40 for a five minute lesson. I haunted the libraries, reading books about Spanish culture and history, and patronized the music shops, buying records and sheet music.

This poem reflects my passion at that time.

Adulthood

Guitars pour out discordant melodies,
a cascading stream of notes ending in flamboyant gesture.
Guitarist's black clothes and flashing dark hands,
pour over strings, faster and faster.

Until.

Quiet passage tremolos up and down,
treble under-toned by deep bass melody.
Girl stands and stamps, and explodes into a fire of dancing.
Castanets click furiously, dress whirling.

She stops.

Clicking quietly, she moves, eyes over shoulder,
cool, dark eyes, shuttered by cool, dark lashes.
Excited male cries "Soleares!"
To the click and clack of castanets,
to the rhythm of pounding feet.

Hands clap and dance,
guitars move up and down,
fingers move furiously fast, and faster notes pouring.
Feet stamping, stamping, hands clapping. Feet stamp!

Ole!

Movements slow,
girl slides tantalizing, from one to another.
Provocative eyes, exciting, cool,
dark, beautiful Moorish woman, bred of gypsies.

Deepened faces watch with dark eyes,
reddened by fire of life
while coals crackle in flickering flame.
Feet whirling, dress flowing.

A stamp!

Adulthood

Tall gaunt man moves out of shadow,
around fire, moving, ever moving.
Guitars tense. He moves slowly to her,
and stares into coal, black eyes.
A proud gesture, you Romany woman.

Gypsy queen.

Fingers whirl and whirl,
hands clap and clap.
Dark figures swaying to dancers, so aloof,
Who gaze at each other.

Dancers stop.

No sound, just guitars and crackling fire.
Melody fades and tension breaks,
crowd rushes forward and embraces.

Dancers kiss.

Laughing faces soften, all is quiet.
Soon, sonorous breathing and crackling coals.

Last Rites

A life altering decision

At the age of twenty, I was exposed to the horrors of World War I through the film, *All Quiet on the Western Front*. It affected me deeply, and I developed the philosophy that when faced with the choice, survival should not come at the cost of humanity.

> A man sits on a hill, a small hill, craters all around.
> His back against a wizened tree that stands seared.
> Stark, upright bark torn and scattered.
> He sits alone, with himself, contemplating.
>
> Projectile whistles overhead, renting the air,
> shuddering the ground into smoky, gas filled clouds.
>
> He gazes into space, unperturbed, and sees
> stars glittering like old friends. Faint recognition.
> Mind grows slow, ever so slow.
>
> Many fires crackle and roar, staccato shots.
> He muses, thinks, understands, with no disturbance of spirit.
>
> Satisfied, he stands ready, waits and senses his being.
>
> Smashed tree lies in the bottom of the crater.
> Mud oozes over wood, where a small hill once stood.

White Witch Virginia

A medium of memory moulded

My mother dabbled in various psychic arts, such as palm reading, the reading of tea leaves, consulting the Ouija board, practising automatic writing, and developing herself as a medium. Through her influence, I was fascinated by extra sensory perception and sought out various mystics while I lived and worked in Brisbane.

At the time, it was illegal to accept payment for a "fortune tell", however, a medium could read palms, tea leaves, crystal balls or engage in other practices, provided that the practitioner inform the subject that they were merely providing entertainment, and could accept a donation for their time.

Elderly females used this loophole to augment their meagre pensions, while socializing with friends. In a café, I met one such woman, a Romany gypsy, who introduced herself as White Witch Virginia. I was twenty years old and fascinated by her, going to see her on a number of occasions over the succeeding weeks. She was astute, sharp, and had an uncanny gift for exposing my personality traits. I enjoyed the interactions immensely and derived great pleasure from my encounters with her.

White Witch Virginia, I played you a song tonight,
White Witch Virginia.
A song of strength and feeling,
a Moorish song, you descendant of Romany.

For you, I would play so many songs, you who I love.
You, who are so powerful, you who inspired, changed.

We met in a café, you told of forthcoming life.
You read me like a book and understood me,
no words to be said.

We were born with it, you said, White Witch Virginia.
So much of you I want to know, to understand,
we people, different from others.

Adulthood

You Romany woman with eyes of fate, with eyes of life.
You'll conquer death, you Romany queen.

So will I, to be with you and your eternal friends.
Tonight, I will see you and tonight we will move mountains.

You destroyed my doubt and I will do it, my Romany woman.
I love you, you ageless person, I love you.

Your face is old, your body weak, but your mind is fine,
White Witch Virginia.
I will meet you again, White Witch Virginia.

Adieu till tonight, White Witch Virginia.

River Bank

The morning after the night before

During my early life, I found maturity did not come to me in a steady progressive way; rather I became emotionally stalled until some profound event or sufficient intellectual and emotional understanding had evolved in my brain, for me to shift to a new level of maturity.

I had been in a relationship with an ex-girlfriend of one of my friends, and my immaturity was condemning it to the ash heap of my social inadequacies.

I underwent one such shift, got up early the next morning, and drove to a fallow field on a bend in the Brisbane River to ponder on its significance.

Warm sun, cool air, clean for a change, and quiet.
People come, and go.
Warm sun pours through warm shirt.

Short grass blades by the river bank, beaten by many feet.
Large schooner floats, idly moving, haphazardly stowed gear.
Trimaran moves slowly up river,
with furled sails and whining motor.

And the little dog stands at the bow.

Black Night

A race to gain perspective

In my research of Spanish culture, I learned of the influence of the "Moor", and encountered the racism that resulted from the mix of different religions. I perceived the value that different cultures bring to the arts, and I was particularly attracted to Flamenco music that was strongly affected by Islamic or "Moorish" culture.

The war is over now, or is it?
And what of the Moors?
Those black and filthy Moors, or are they?

Five dark faces sit silently around the casket,
black garments still as they murmur.
Solitary candle flickers feebly, fighting the air
and throwing ghastly light on long-dead face.

Deadly notes strike the air, the foul air.
Polished guitar reflects faint light,
illuminating a guitarist's gaunt face,
while the cold casket sits silently in shadow.

Night on the Beach

Extending life into regions of memory

In another of my sojourns on Alexandria Beach, I became engaged in deep listening, deep feeling, and deeper thinking.

Last few flames flickers feebly, white ash settles on log.
"Tis night, Tis night," screech the eugary bird.
"I know" smile I.

Blackness creeps up, fire glare holds it back.
Smoke dazes my eyes as I remember other camp fires,
small fires, embers dull and red.

Roaring blazes, love expressed through tinkering of guitars,
and mouth organs, moaning melancholy,
singing soft, swaying to the flames.

Quiet night, pieces of clouds grid the stars
that look through their unfinished roof.

Wind cools my hair,
and my face is hot.

Life

Theme and contrast

I can jump, I can leap, I can bound,
I can spring into the cold, crisp, frosty air,
with my breath punctuating the stillness
of the expanding dawn.

How I love life!
Not always, but mostly.

Sometimes, I drape myself over a chair,
and crumple my face in quivering hands,
wet with the salt of life's pain.

Sometimes, I slump my shoulders into an old jacket,
and drag my feet into procrastination.

Sometimes, just sometimes,
injustice flays me into submission,
while the sun turns white, and drained colour
blackens trees and flowers.

A Day in Spain

Life repeated and love enveloped

After playing one of my Flamenco pieces at a concert and describing a scene in Andalucía, I was asked by one of the audience about my travels in Spain. They were quite surprised when I told them that I had never visited the country. My passion for the music had driven me to soak up as much literary reference to the country that I could find.

> The sun was hot, the day quiet.
> Old man leans against the stone wall,
> big sombrero masking him.
>
> Down the dry dusty rows, a cemetery of houses,
> gaunt and stark against the breathless sky.
> Little dog panting softly.
>
> Baby moans quietly as the red dust lay all about,
> while the hot, hated sun mocked overhead. People sleep.
>
> Dog padded softly away, as three faces of youth
> popped from an old rust-lined rain barrel,
> and chuckled a laugh that rippled the red dust.
>
> In a dirt stained corner, an ancient face
> peered from under the black shade.
> White handkerchief flashed.
>
> Children ran laughing down the dirty street,
> dogs barking at their heels, with rising dust
> choking the flies.
>
> ***
>
> Old man stirred, stretched,
> and stood from the old floor boards.
> Voices became thunderous, and amid the tumult,
> came the bark of dog.

Adulthood

Men began to work, blacksmiths struck,
carpenter called to apprentice, bright and bold.

***

Sweated and stained, they went to their homes of stone,
where click of tongue and sparkle of eye,
delighted their partner of love.

Bloody orb of sun, cut into distant crags,
and breeze moved ragged curtains.
Light of day softened, and eased their hearts.

***

Sharp from the plaza,
a cascade of notes to a girl leaning from balcony.
Guitar flowed and moved, as she breathed a sigh.

Rich voice softly sang of love, deep love.
Singing lowered with passing light, soon neither.

In youthful night he stood, a statue,
guitar in one hand, lover in other.
Curtains moved and they too.
Flesh touched flesh.

***

Arm, strong and lithe, lay flung back across the bed,
that supple body, collapsed, exhausted, slept.

Her legs entwined, face upon chest, they slept.
All slept, to meet the next day with strength.

Maturity

The Race

Run to live and live to run

Once a year, a local running club sponsored a two day relay race from Courtenay to Victoria on the west coast of Canada. Around 120, ten-member teams from North America, competed in the approximately 230 kilometer-long race over the Victoria Day long weekend. Teams with bizarre names and uniforms made the event an exciting and companionable one.

This poem is about the start of the race.

Yellow neon cuts through chinks of motel armour,
I feel my skin enveloped in strange cloth.
Coal-fire red pokes my eyes out of mystery.
Three-fifty…Ten minutes more.

Scattered around me in grey habit,
my companions breathe in the swish of a car,
sliding the asphalt ribbon into Night's maw.

I ponder their peace, faces upturned in softness.
Bones crack, I emerge from my cocoon,
siding my hot skin into cold, velvet air.

"What time is it?"
A query whispered across fathoms of friendship.
An answer echoes over the canyon of cave.

I reach the bathroom, and hesitate
to burn my brain with stubbled recognition.
I force the switch into submission,
and squint at life's damage.

Maturity

Water sloshes my cheeks,
bringing life to my heart,
while the worms of dread,
wriggle in the abyss of gut.
I drink, and nectar slips through me.

On the shelf, lies the uniform of my desires.
Bold team colours flush my skin with pride,
as I don the persona of long-forgotten warriors.

Outside, cold oxygen permeates my lungs.
Voices change into sonorous rumbles,
amid swishing nylon and clapping doors.

Others fret their way, back and forth,
from hive to vehicle.
Acrid fumes flare my nostrils,
the lumpy bag heaved into gaping trunk.

"So this is it, huh!"
"Yeah."
"How do you feel?"
"Lousy."
"Hey, do us a favour will you, Bob,
get my hands around a coffee."
"Nothing's open. Here, have some apple juice."

I suck the plastic straw,
drawing the sweet juice into budding taste.

Through the dew laced windscreen,
a banner accelerates into vision,
proclaiming the start of my adventure.

Skylight brightens the crowd of moving flesh,
as I ease my bones into extension
to reach into the air above.

Creeping up on an innocent horizon,
the impatient sun lies ready to pounce,
golden fur exposing its position to the wary.

Maturity

A team of red and black whisks past.
"...so what did he do?"
"Paid it, he had to y'know. What could he do..."
Softening sounds smoothing into symphonic silence.

I stretch my limbs, draping my bare arms
over the emanating energy of engine.

I feel steady again, a little nervous, a little shy.
A little child again, eager for the rush of wind,
eager for bare feet pounding
to the vision of unsteady goal posts,
looming through sweat stained brows.

Time to move.

My friends crowd me, a palm strikes my shoulder.
A warm kiss on my cheek to expose the flush of feeling.

I move to Courtenay's banner,
mingling secretively with the chosen ones,
awaiting my fate by the gods of chemistry.

I am hailed, I am cajoled to be proper,
to conduct myself with honour and dignity,
to feel pleasure in this brevity of existence.

I am distracted, I dream a while,
then fret myself back to the present.

My wrist twists into view,
a poised finger hovers over the beginning of time,
waiting to launch me into being.

A shock of sound, a surge.
Life rushes my veins to solve the puzzle of flashing heels.

The maze of Lycra fish,
swimming in a sea of anticipation,
darts me over puddles and painted lines,
and a burst makes me free.

Maturity

I drink in sweet oils from opening blooms,
while my drumming heart,
steadies to the baton of my lungs.
I rest my soul and plan my future.

Around the encroaching bend,
a stretch of bobbing heads leads me on,
through cottages, shrubs,
and into a severed forest of giant Douglas Firs,
who shadow their way across the cold, tar trail.

"Looking good!"
"Keep it up!"
"Y're doin' well so far."

A knowing hand thrusts the bottle to fumbling grasp.
Between rasps, I draw the fluid past dry tongue.

"How far?" I blurt.
"Just two kay to go."
"You're goin' great."
"See you at the exchange."

My hand gestures reply, as he peels off me,
exposing my loneliness to the faceless shirt ahead.
I push my tired frame to close the separation.
He looms larger, until I brush his damp shoulder.

"Good work."
I slide the phrase out of mouth corner,
breathing past with challenged passion.

I smell the end, and bend the corner
to follow Marshall's pointed finger.

I see them all,
I see the crowds,
I see the end,
I see the opening, waiting for lasting struggle.

Maturity

I see my friend,
hand outstretched in greeting,
she leans ahead to escape my exhausted staggers
and strikes my hand.
She is gone, sucked up in a confusion of colour.

I walk to the sun,
sensing its growing warmth.
I breath off miles.

My team crowds me, their eager eyes search my face,
absorbing my moments of experience.

The question is last asked.
"So, how was it?"
"Piece o' cake!"

Southern Ocean

A young man and his sea

In 1984, I set sail in my thirty-two foot sloop, Laiviṇa, to achieve a non-stop solo circumnavigate the globe. After rounding Cape Horn at the southern tip of South America, Laiviṇa travelled an easterly course along the fiftieth parallel of latitude towards Australia. Approaching Île Kerguélen, to the north of Antarctica, a powerful storm hit the little vessel.[3]

It was such a state, when I tempted fate,
the year I sought to roam.
I was in a place, so full of grace,
that had now become my home.

My little boat, so strong and blessed,
had taken me so far south.
The wind blew hard from the nor'west,
the sails so tight in its mouth.

Near the ice and through the fog,
for days we surged along.
No sun to sight, no track to log,
just the albatross, with wings so strong.

The pressure dropped, the wind backed nigh,
the fog it thinned to show
a tortured sky, the mares tails high,
and it really began to blow.

The night came on, the stars they shone,
and my sextant snatched a sight.
Up ahead, to my dread,
lay an island, with ice so white.

---

[3] *Cape Horn Birthday*: ISBN-10: 1948494043; ISBN-13: 978-1948494045 by Seaworthy Publications Inc.

Maturity

I changed my course, to open sea,
southward I would go.
There lay a rock, in my lee,
that added to my woe.

The main it tore, from luff to leach,
the remnants flogging hard.
I took it in, less some of my skin,
yard by weary yard.

Without a sail, bare poles to the sky,
I lashed the tiller down.
My boat would drift, by and by,
I hoped I would not drown.

The water cold, the ice so near,
the dark a funeral gown.
The rigging screamed as if to fear
the mast would crash on down.

I lashed my body to rails so hard,
the cold cut to my core.
Sea shanties I did sing,
my spirits would raise, I swore.

Midnight came and an hour went,
the cold was so intense.
I'd go below, some food I meant,
to help me make some sense.

Before I moved, a roar so loud,
behind me, it came.
I clung in dread, my body cowed,
as I braced against the frame.

A watery punch, like a pile,
knocked us in a heap.
My little boat, it fell a mile
'till the mast had buried deep.

Maturity

I held my breath in waters greyed,
my lungs so ached for air.
Upside down, my boat it stayed,
until I coaxed a desperate prayer.

A shudder felt, an unseen hand
had turned us from our tomb.
The mast rose up and pointed high,
a first cold gasp outside a womb.

The hollow mast, it drained its load,
of ocean so very deep.
The fluorescent glow, away it flowed,
until the dark was so complete.

The hours crept by until I spied
a grey dawn easing sweet.
At first ten yards, then a mile,
an alien world I did greet.

The sea I saw was covered wide
with white foam a metre thick.
The wind it plowed through the froth,
leaving furrows long and slick.

Between the swells, quiet for a spell,
until a hill came near.
I lifted up and from high aloft,
I came to see my fear.

Far away, and below my feet,
lay a valley so deep and wide.
The rolling hills so swift and fleet,
took it in its stride.

The sun came down, and the wind it slowed
and I felt my spirits leap.
I took the sign to be benign,
and fell into a blissful sleep.

Maturity

When I awoke, the day was new,
the sun it kissed the sea.
I set some sail and headed east,
I once again was free.

Passage

Passion, purpose and persistence

After crossing the equator and fighting through the Doldrums on my homeward leg, Laiviṇa picked up the northeast trade winds and we settled down to life at sea.[4]

I lay on my back on a cool hard deck,
with the star pierced night poised above.
The Southern Cross stood on the horizon
while the Hunter attacked from high.

A cool air brushed my bare chest,
hardening me with its fingers,
mixing with warm exhalations
as it slid into tossed foam.

White ghost sails purred and surged,
thrusting with purpose,
sliding my sleek shining ship
into parted and waiting waves of joy

Of exaltation.
Of experience.

Wetness touched me,
clinging with comfort,
drying coolly in the aging night.

---

4 *Blackberries* - Poems from the Salt Spring Library Open Mic"

Expression

Eternal musing

Forever pondering the meaning of life and not willing to accept that I have the answer.

>Do poets...and I count myself
>as one of few, and few of many,
>bring life to the living,
>and touch heart to the beating?
>
>Do we...or they, hurt us
>with their pain, their struggle,
>and spirit of love all full and true,
>demand our time to record their woe?
>
>Are we...yes, I know my kin,
>mere scribes and scribblers of other riches,
>historians of the heart,
>not purveyors of passion?
>
>Is poetry...like beauty and love,
>inside the marbled stone
>awaiting our chisel
>to remove the burden over its glow?
>
>Will I...and others, fore and aft,
>reach a destination of soul,
>a port of calling,
>built by strangers?
>
>Will we ever...in our lifetime,
>know our fellow, our friend in blood,
>our legacy and duty,
>to bond in secret tryst?

Maturity

I hope…yes, I yearn,
to know these answers many,
for what are we then,
surely not flesh upon a frame?

Time…that murderous beast
that severs before we meet
on hallowed ground to share again
our dreams of life and love.

But time…the fiend we fear,
is but a friend, a surprise to some,
that wields a weapon so potent,
and builds an arch of connection.

It struts…between the ages,
and connects us, all and sundry,
with generations past, long dead now,
to share our human condition.

Yes…its moving pen has writ,
their lines live on and on and on,
to bring beauty and truth from dusty realms,
and tears to wash us pure.

Lover's Call

To be human, is to love with passionate embrace

Of all the human emotions, love is the most complex and the most powerful. The physical expression of love binds us together in ways that defy explanation.

That ribbon entwining my self with feeling,
love that makes with you, my essence.
A winding trail with ups and down,
my body, your body, our body.

Sometimes, my dominance seizes you in its grasp,
yet my submission gives you pleasure.
Life, love, and joyful exuberance,
that takes me to my knees.

I feel your response, so rich and pure,
wash over me, a warm ocean swell,
full of life, smooth and evolving,
cascading down my hardening body.

With my eyes, I see your shape,
that exquisite, beautiful form,
so feminine, so exotic, so alive,
flowing sensually over movement and desire.

I see your breasts, your hips, your thighs,
firmness rounding over legs
that curl and slide upon the sheets,
and arms that bring me to you.

My hands trace your outline,
fingers coursing over soft skin,
sensing your response within,
and expressing my desire without.

Maturity

Fingertips rippling slowly
over fibres of feminine feeling,
collecting crumbs of sensuous repast,
and tasting the passion flower.

I take it in, I take it all in,
breathed in with the scent of pleasure,
the taste of anticipation,
the siren sound of sation.

I take you in, and bury you deep
into my soul, my being, my self,
and my heart it swells, and washes me
with life, living lustily.

I draw you to me, all of you,
with no boundaries and no resistance.
I draw me to you with no regrets,
rushing into love's tight embrace.

The crashing wave, the elixir of love,
dominates our spirit, and binds our bodies
in exhaustive experience, again and again,
until your love conquers my lust.

I am left with sleep awashed,
awakened only by the tenderness of touch,
the fleet of feeling,
and the sound of sensation.

Touch

Nursed from damage to design

On April 3, 2017, I was cycling home after a training ride one afternoon, and descending the long steep hill into the town of Ganges on Salt Spring Island. Coming up the hill, driving a car, was a middle aged woman with her daughter and grandson as passengers. She reached the spot just opposite her daughter's house, turned the car to cross the road, and enter the driveway. I was descending the hill at a speed of about forty-five kilometres an hour, when suddenly I saw the car cut across my lane, right in front of me. There was no time to brake, only time to scream, "Don't turn!"

When I became aware of my surroundings, it was dark, and I was lying on a hospital bed, with a surgeon hovering over me. He explained that the impact had driven my right femur back and shattered my hip socket. The front of my left calf muscle had been degloved from my leg going into the front right wheel-well of the car.

I spent the next month recuperating in the hospital, before going home in a wheel chair. Eventually, I graduated to crutches, and then to walking sticks. Finally, after a year, I was running and bicycling again.

While lying on my back in the hospital, I wrote this poem.

The pre-dawn fog of pain
swirled through the hills
and valleys of my broken flesh.

I sought clarity of existence
from the night of incandescent hurt
that narrowed my world to slivers.

No longing, no yearning,
I sought no thing,
except the oblivion of sleep.

Touch, my fleshless weakened arm felt
your touch enveloping my wrist,
feeling my life through your fingers.

Maturity

The tightening cuff, a focus
of pressure, and a world beyond
my darkened eyelids.

A scent behind, and again alone,
a wrinkled sheet, damp and coarse,
the plane of my existence.

***

A later time, a newer world,
a bright clarity of thought,
all consumed in rich awareness.

Sounds, scents, colours, and tasting
my expanding health and life,
now so full, so gregarious.

Touch, my firm fingers wrapped
my touch around your hand,
feeling your care of giving.

Returning what you gave
freely to my vulnerable,
your succour to my sorrow.

Relation of Being

A flash before eyes of old

Connecting all of my years of life into one moment in time, and putting it instantly into context.

Smooth my way before me,
as I flow my life ahead.
Time takes me by my hands,
to lead me to its dance.

Warmth of life, burnt with passion,
charges into my soul so fast,
propelling me to the place
destined for my kin and me to cherish.

Colours fresh from their ripening,
washes the wounds of my errors
and restore me to my being,
to connect me to the living.

Wet with the thunderstorm of youth,
drenching my eyes with tears
of regret, of loss, of lives not lived,
as I walk the path that binds me tight.

I would not have it any other way,
this world of knowing and wondering.
A place, my place, in the shine
of your love and my deep remorse.

Wisdom

A Gathering of Vanished Days

In remembrance of our errors

Regrets. We all have regrets. Perhaps we have inadvertently breathed life into the errors of our ways; we should not condemn ourselves for our transgressions.

In the gloom of forest deep,
I came upon a gathering a-creep.
I saw them there and knew them well,
for they were mine before I fell.

My lost days so very ill-spent,
were here before me, all broken and bent.
They watched me now, with intrigue and ware,
as I entered their circle on a dare.

"Why do you meet?" I ventured bold,
"To share your secrets," I was told.
"But you are lost!" I proclaimed.
"Not to us, for we are reclaimed."

"You are our creator, our birth,
for that we are glad," said the first.
I studied them with growing dread,
for they all knew where my life had led.

I wish I could but change those days,
but time had taken them in devious ways.
"You are mine, yet you do not belong.
Have I done you such a great wrong?"

Wisdom

"Concern yourself not, for we now exist
and share with you, a life you kissed.
We days may not have been your best,
yet we together may finally rest."

I stood there amid the litter,
and watched my days no longer bitter.
They all joined hands and began to dance,
around they went, I became entranced.

When I awoke, I was all alone.
The sun had set, and I had known
I could now leave this place,
with understanding and grace.

For I had loved, lived and lost,
yet in my heart, I had not tossed
those days I seized so youthfully,
and discarded so cavalierly.

Growth

The passage of a life of movement

The many chapters of life and experience expressed in the Ghazal form.

A wail of first breath pierces the air,
his bottom spanked by the hand not holding his legs.

On his feet, he totters along, splatting the floor,
the enticing toy coming ever closer to his little legs.

Pump arms and breath deeply the fresh sweet morn.
Grass under feet while dead stalks brush flying legs.

Quick! Stop the car! Fast comes the danger.
Thrust his foot to hit the brakes, a tremor up his legs.

Walking down the aisle, arm around his bride,
stiff body planted in shiny shoes and trousers brushing legs.

Along the path, the crutches under arm press,
scissoring the warm air around his plastered legs.

He sits on his narrow scooter, with its electric motor,
passing through aisles, with groceries on his legs.

The wooden box sits on the cradle, soft silk and fabric.
Peter lies unmoved with the cushions against his legs.

A Heart of Changes

A love that speaks not its name

Australia, like many other English speaking countries in the 1950's and 1960's, had laws against homosexuality and was a challenging time for LGBTQ people. While lesbians were tolerated, gays were not, incurring many derogatory names. In Australia, around the time of my youth, gays were commonly referred to as "Poofters." My quiet and sensitive nature had earned me the nickname of "Poofter Pete".

The abuse that infected my soul from an early age left me emotionally confused about love and sex. It has taken many decades of work to rebuild myself closer to what I should have been.

I heard the taunts, the slurs,
the force of hate, direct and intense.
So young, so hurt, so complicit.

Who were they, these people,
so different, so despised, so needing
of love, that they dared break our rules.

In the street, they chose to hold hands,
and walk so bold, so brave,
while I stood by so puzzled.

But I was young, and my change
had not come, until a friend,
a dear friend, had left me in haste.

The hurt I felt, was this love?
The same, when my longing strong
for one so opposite, now the same?

We had touched, had closed,
had taken into an embrace,
a world of something I before had not felt.

Wisdom

Something had grown, unknown to me,
that seemed so sure, so right, but oh
the shock of loss too much to bear.

And with it came the pain, the guilt,
thrust from the knowing world
into the dark of my youthful fears.

I came with much trepidation
into the place of my new kin,
and there I met a man of depth.

Charged with fear and courage both,
I apprenticed my body to him,
and learned my hope of another life.

A journeyman now, I trod my way deep in thought,
to resolve the dilemma
and ambiguity of my self.

Yet, the years between, and further I fled
from understanding, a complete self
staved off by time and design.

But now, I purpose myself
to grow beyond my fear, beyond my fate,
and seize this challenge a final time.

And with hope, that wherever it takes,
I will be true, and test the bounds
of my self induced affection.

For all humanity, for all peoples
that care for others as I carry my care,
into respect and recognition.

Boys Will Be Boys

Manhood's toxic legacy

The explosion of revelations that proceeded from the exposure of many powerful males in our unbalanced society, caused me to examine my life and the damaging cultural influences I had to excise from my psyche. At last, women have gained courage and seized power, and are speaking out. Now men must do the same.

Boys will be boys,
but whose will was it
that propelled me into this world
of social inequity and confusion.

Who was I? A blank slate
upon which you could write,
to imprint me with misogyny
and further your aims and disguise.

I saw the difference,
so easily embraced by my sex,
that gave us power
at her expense.

Where were you?
When my confusion intuited a response,
an explanation to ease my thoughts,
as I adopted you mores.

But where were the others?
Those nascent scents
to heal my soul
and succour my love?

So I lived within me,
and saw the other,
shadowy figures that moved as I,
the same, the very same.

Wisdom

Yet so undeserving
of my life, the same?
Why not…yes, and why not?
How could this be?

How could I bond? Really bond
with my companion creature,
when an alien gulf
perpetuated self in extreme?

How could I enjoy
those benefits given me,
when she was left
a powerless house?

It must end now,
we must be, truly be,
alive to our co-joined life
of living bold, and yet in space.

A reflection of meaning,
of purpose beyond our petty world,
that makes us love, to live
for love, for life.

Then it came,
as in a rush
of bubbled memories
to my surface calm.

Oh, the rage of loss,
this must not be!
My guilt held me fast
until it too, lost to love.

Of my bondswoman,
of all that life, doubly so.
My kin and I, what had we missed?
A path of life ripped from us both.

Wisdom

I have seen, some others
take a stance and say it aloud,
the beast, in this tiny room,
can not, must not be allowed.

To rape amok and left fly
those wolves of their desire,
demand, while I stand by,
so idle in my comfort and grace.

They must face, they will face
the wrath of many,
to plunge a spear,
and disperse their chimera.

To drive our wedge
into the cracks of their edifice,
and let not our pathos
turn us from our path.

We should not cease
our incense potent
before all this hate is gone.
Forever…we must!

Unfulfilled

Blind yearnings of invisible passion

There is a fine line between solitude and loneliness. When that border is overstepped, one needs to capture the strength of feeling from being alone, and appreciate it for its richness. This is preferable to seeing it as a debilitating force that threatens to rob one of all spirit.

Is it too much to ask, as I lie alone
and my body craves that touch
that opens my spirit to the brightening dawn
of my saddened life.

Is it really that much, that I must do
more than what I need ask of myself
in these troubling years of decayed pretense,
that robs me of my passionate glow.

Oh, I would that I could but take myself
into a soft and gentle embrace
with one of laughter, rich and resonant,
to soothe my ache of heartless love.

For you, I would carry myself from friends so bold,
into a world of stark refresh and senses deep.
And you, I take into my depths with care,
to create a bond so vigorous strong.

To last for eons, long and drawn,
as all of us yearn, during nights too cold
for weakened contemplation of fleshy pursuits,
that drive our distractions to despair.

I am but one of many, whose time may come
to take this dilemma in its sharpened horn,
and pierce the wanton suffering of my poor self,
in my relief of passion upon barren cloth.

Wisdom

And will it be right, this choice of mine,
to run amok amid such changeling times,
that test the pursuit of many goals,
and yet may fall upon such stagnant ground.

I do not know, yet persist I must,
to climb that monstrous peak
against agonized contempt of all around,
to breath my soul into loving life.

Melancholy

Ranging the emotional prairie

One challenge of the creative mind is to endure the polar opposite of what gives it its force and power. The theme of life must exist with contrasts and one must bear those opposites with understanding and knowledge of their importance.

I knew my purpose, long and sinuous,
from its cradle to my gravity of living,
shackled and bounding fresh into a liberty
ripped from my mother's wounded past.

I presented my second coming upon a puzzled crowd,
to be judged by my peerless resolve to be,
or not to question what came first,
that chickened spirit or its rotted offspring.

I leaned into a blind force of willing,
to move my psychic connection
beyond where my being dreaded,
its feet locked into concrete surety.

For gales of loving, break silently
upon my stony beach of shingled hide,
where I seek that truth, and nothing but the conviction
I need to bind a path to my crooked resolve.

Moulded into stain for you to discard,
bad and unwanted when unneeded,
I see the light at that endless turning,
driving my passion unabated.

Yet there is that beast within the room,
rearing its fear of ugly minds,
spinning in their craven solitude,
to judge or be lost to all.

Wisdom

I do not know what I shall become,
from now until that eternity of silence,
deadens the pulse that guides my spirit,
and reaches into the heart of childish rapture.

Oh, to reach, to hold, to seize the living daylights,
and squeeze the stuff from the very fabric of soul,
weaving my life into its nature of existing,
to drape my aching heart with shuttered sadness.

But where is the heat from within, to boil a movement
so strong, as to burst through the belt of banality,
and push me from the edge, into a commune with all,
and sun drenched hopeful symphonic reason.

Memory and patience, guides from the ages of before,
hold wise and sage council, and with time,
I can become a paragon of virtue in kind.
With hope, I will share my common tragedy.

Four Horsemen

A modern metropolis of mendacious meddling

In attempting to coalesce the reasons for the plague of ills that beset the world, I seized on the Four Horsemen of the Apocalypse as my inspiration.

Might is again right,
or has it just left us
struggling to regain
the humanity of our spirit?

We gave our power freely,
with expectations
that others would share theirs,
instead of such vile accumulations.

Should we also scrabble
in the filth of greed,
like our privileged kin,
to take what little remains?

I hear the hooves of horses
thundering toward our meek inheritance.
Our apocalypse now in sight
of those four, deadly demons unleashed.

Political power has been taken
so insidiously and completely,
that our tainted house guests
defend their demands against us.

Financial power robs us of food
and the water of life-giving need,
swapped for tools of control
to steal our thoughtful soul.

Wisdom

Military power attacks our bodies
from invisible heights
with such callous precision
to further their elite aims.

Language power has taken our voice
and weakened its strident prophesy.
A mouse among the media lions,
stomped in their pride.

But they know their weakness,
and they fear the power of poets.
The language of lyrics and the voice of value
that pours through the music of life.

I yearn for a peace of people just,
that share my friends with care and attention,
given with honour accepted,
and ideas cast among fertile fields.

I strive for the power to halt those beasts
that overtake our quest to sustain.
Translucent beauty meandering through forest cool,
and tumbling over passions slow.

I fight for the right to spring
our treasured children into seasoned summer,
and let us fall, our duties made,
to winter our discontent.

Apocalypse

Whose future will be given?

The frustration that my friends feel for the apathy that exists at a time when our whole world should be in an uproar over the vast and systemic injustice foisted on the innocent, inspired me to articulate this shared instinct.

I'm tired of people
following like sheep,
and herding their instinct into logic
convoluted by times renewed.

We lose our selves into landscapes
devoid of artless review,
and prosaic feeling
sculpted from colourless kitsch.

What to do, and what can we do,
as we run round a chicken
with our head deep in the soil of turmoil,
ploughed under our furrowed brow.

Darkness forces its way
with us, a willing accomplice
to the tyranny of the few remaining vestiges of sanity
that lie doggedly sleeping.

Where is our lifeline
cast upon muddied waters,
and stirred from a pot blackened and kettled
into the rage of youthful indiscretion.

How do we grow on a shrinking world
of thawed surmises, that rarely solidify
into actions that we can collect,
and take into our children's heart and soul.

Wisdom

To wind their crying presence
into such a ball of contention,
that they grasp at the straw men
who populate those places of power.

Oh, how I long for some change
of pacing my strident clamour,
to reach the very heart and sole endeavour
that rewards an enduring sense of feeling.

Quietly, we can still take each other into arms
that soften the ill wind blowing
across vast reaches of discordant civility,
to shake our founding to its suspicious core.

Unite the dark and moon burst glow upon my fever,
rob me of my pain, and suffer the children of my words,
for they are my budding offspring,
who leap me into graceful poise.

Future Shock

Retaining humanity through thick and thin

World politics, the climate crisis, the widening wealth gap, refugees fleeing war, famine, and hatred, along with the many other ills of our modern world, inspired me to express the turmoil that infects my spirit.

I took my soul into that darkened hole,
of timeless and ill repute.
When men were bold and life so old,
and women so very mute.

I don't belong, and yet I long
for a bond that breaks the chains.
When shackles bright in the deepened night,
fall from my sickened brain.

It is, I think, as my heart does sink,
a world that has lost is way.
Yet all around in city and town,
is a beauty of life in sway.

What steals our time in its pristine prime,
and condemns it to history's heap.
It robs our might, through our fright,
of fears that makes us sheep.

A fate now clear, affects our sphere,
too late to make a stand.
Yet we must haste to reduce our waste,
and scream our sentient demand.

All we have fought may come to naught
if we do but let it go.
Not text, not quotes, but voice from throats
is the power we can bestow.

Wisdom

Yet in the mist of words we kissed,
when we sought to touch our kin,
lies a love of life through all this strife,
and humanity to pull within.

We must prevail to tell our tale,
to children for their sake.
Our legacy so poor, is but a spoor
upon a dried out lake.

I will commit to do my bit,
As all should do their part.
When hard times come and hope is glum,
I'll be true and keep my heart.

Friend

The innocence of youth

I was strolling with my wife on the beach at Cadboro Bay when we saw two young teenage girls walking together. They were holding hands and enjoying each other's company. I was touched by the display of friendship I saw, so I wrote this poem. I imagined them at a different beach, Long Beach, Tofino, where there are wide expanses of sand and powerful breaking waves in a relatively undeveloped region.

Beach sand pushed up between my toes,
thrilling my awaking love
of your spirit of connection.

A folding wave, trapped living breath
that caught your eyes aglow with sun drenched movement
of wheeling bird.

An aging day faced us each together,
to seek meaning in your queried face,
tilted head, and enigmatic smile.

Is it this place of life that taught my spirit
of friendship, to go beyond my need
to feel the flowing water swirl my ankles?

Was it your eyes that sought mine,
or was it your finger that traced a line along my palm
and expanded my heart beneath my swelling breast?

I felt our years of friendship coalesce
into a new bond of us that I had taken so freely,
and now gently, with your hand holding mine.

Where did it come from? I had no idea,
but I cherished the soft sea air
brushing your hair from your face.

Wisdom

I felt my tongue move a kiss onto my lips,
to await a time when I would send my soul
to your heart, my friend, my deep friend.

How much can I take
of richness exploding from my being,
knowing you so softly close to our beginning.

I dare not speak and break the spell
that binds us to this place
and its time of knowing.

I feel the softening light pass over your outstretched arms,
embracing our moment of salty tang,
and binding our touch of skin.

You turned to the dunes and I caught your waist,
to rest my trembling chin
upon your bare shoulder.

And a tear of mine descended to your neck
to bring life and growth, and what I can
to you, my friend.

Images

Image	Page	Details	Credit
	F	Eden, Little Cove, Noosa Heads	Mary Freeman
	iv	Sand Formation, Beekeepers Nature Reserve, Western Australia	Peter Freeman
	vi	Arvita with Candle	Peter Freeman
	42	Salvation Army Home for Men, Stanley Street, Brisbane (Negative # 6547)	State Library of Queensland
	44	West Head, Malborough Sounds, New Zealand	Peter Freeman
	49	South Alexandria Bay, Noosa Heads	Peter Freeman
	52	Lake Wabby, Fraser Island, Dec 1989	Peter Freeman
	66	Potato Slough, Sacramento River, California	Peter Freeman

Images

Image	Page	Details	Credit
	68	Glowing Coals, Salt Spring Island	Peter Freeman
	69	Coastal Cycleway, Mandurah	Peter Freeman
	76	2003 M50 400m Finals, Carolina, Puerto Rico	Peter Freeman
	80	Laiviṇa east of the Falkland Islands	Peter Freeman
	84	Wendy, Lake Wabby, Fraser Island	Peter Freeman
	89	Arbutus and Douglas Fir, Musgrave Landing, Salt Spring Island	Peter Freeman
	108	Shannon and Stephanie, Nicola Lake, BC, Canada	Peter Freeman
	B	Sunrise through fog, Victoria, BC, Canada	Peter Freeman

About the Author

Peter Freeman lives on Salt Spring Island on the west coast of Canada. He writes non-fiction and fictional novels, children's books, screen and stage plays, short stories, magazine articles, and poetry.

He grew up in what was once the sleepy, fishing village of Noosa Heads on the Sunshine Coast, just south of the Great Barrier Reef, Australia. He started his working career first as a cadet surveyor, then a journeyman fitter and turner, and finally focused on computer science at the University of Tasmania.

While in Hobart, Peter joined the local rock-climbing club where he later met Max Dorfligger, a carpenter, shipwright and famous Swiss mountaineer. Peter sailed across the Tasman Sea to New Zealand with Max in the thirty-two foot sloop, *Sunshine*, that Max had built. Peter then spent the next few years in Dunedin as a train driver and building his own sailboat, *Laiviṇa*.

Peter sailed from New Zealand to Australia and then onto Canada where he incorporated an Information Technology company (Southern Cross Systems Ltd.), producing and selling scientific and business software to universities, government and the private sector.

In 1984, Peter departed Victoria, British Columbia, to sail his thirty-two foot sloop, *Laiviṇa*, on a solo non-stop circumnavigation of the globe, breaking the existing world record in a time of 236 days. His book, *Cape Horn Birthday*, is an account of this journey.

About the Author

Representing Canada in world championships, Peter competed as a masters athlete in Italy, South Africa, Australia, the USA, and Canada, and has won gold, silver and bronze medals from these competitions in the 100, 200, 400, and 800 metre events. In 2003, Peter was ranked 11th in the world and 1st in Canada for his 55.10 second time in the 400 metres.

As a keen cyclist, Peter has twice ridden his bicycle across Canada. Without any support, he took 79 bicycling days to cover the 15,400 kilometre perimeter of Australia, averaging 200 kilometres a day.

Peter sums up his philosophy of life in the last paragraph of his book, *Cape Horn Birthday*:

> We truly know ourselves and our world when we know our limits. As we gain experience by going close to our limits and thus get to know ourselves better, that experience moves our limits further away. This leaves us with the conundrum of never really knowing ourselves yet knowing ourselves intimately...because we kissed the lips of eternity and breathed the air of existence.[5]

---

5 *Cape Horn Birthday:* ISBN-10: 1948494043; ISBN-13: 978-1948494045

www.ingramcontent.com/pod-product-compliance
Lightning Source LLC
Chambersburg PA
CBHW032233080426
42735CB00008B/829